CW01522123

THE

AONAĊ ΤΑΙΙΤΕΑΝΝ

AND

THE TAILTEANN GAMES

*THEIR ORIGIN
HISTORY AND ANCIENT
ASSOCIATIONS*

By T. H. NALLY

DUBLIN
THE TALBOT PRESS LIMITED
LONDON
T. FISHER UNWIN, LIMITED

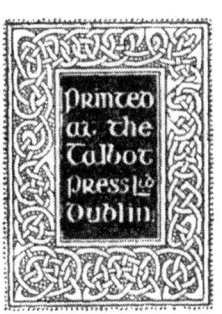

Printed at the Talbot Press Ltd Dublin

CONTENTS

INTRODUCTION.

THIS story of the historic games of Ancient Ireland has been compiled with a view to familiarising the Irish people with a knowledge, however imperfect, of their ancient greatness in the Athletic World.

It is surely something to be proud of to know that our country has played a great and noble part in the Past, not merely in leading all the nations of Europe in intellectual culture and the higher arts of civilization, but also in the no less important province of physical development.

Most Irish people know how distinguished their nation once was in the world of letters, when the great men of the world flocked to our shores for light and learning, but few of our people to-day, we fear, can claim a knowledge even as intimate with our ancient history as that shown by an eminent foreign writer who states :

7

" Indeed, so far as history is concerned, Ireland boasts of by far the most ancient organised sports known, *i.e.*, the Tailteann Games, or (as he also calls them) *Lugnasad*."

It is surely something to our credit to have even this much admitted by a hostile writer, who, at the same time, confesses that anything even vaguely approaching organised sports was quite unknown in England until long after the Norman invasion, "when the nobles, for the first time, devoted themselves to the chase and the joust, while the people played games of ball on the village green."

The chroniclers of succeeding centuries are silent concerning any athletic exercises more exciting in England than mere training for war. It is true, it is recorded that Henry V. (A.D. 1413) and two of his lords ran fast enough to catch a wild buck in an open park; but Edward III., a little earlier, actually prohibited weight-putting by statute.

So small was the attention given to physical development and sports generally in England in A.D. 1509, that Richard Pace, the Secretary of Henry VIII., advised the sons of the noblemen to " leave study and learning to the children of the meaner people and practise their sports."

In Ireland, on the other hand, learning and physical exercises went hand-in-hand from times long beyond chronological history.

It is with a desire to recall such facts to the minds of our race that this little book has been written, in the hope that it may help to awaken once more a deeper interest in our glorious past, and assist, in a small way, in restoring some of the ancient athletic fame achieved by the Tailteann Games.

T. H. N.

The "Aonaċ Tailteann"
AND
THE TAILTEANN GAMES

Their Origin, History, and Ancient Associations

THE adoption of the ancient historic title, "Aonaċ Tailteann," as a suitable name to characterise Ireland's great National Festival this year, and to distinguish it from all others of its kind in any part of the world, was not only a happy inspiration, but, at the present juncture, a singularly appropriate one.

As originally established, away back in the nebulous mists that envelop the outer edges of chronological history—almost two thousand years before the birth of Christ—the Tailteann Games were primarily instituted as a tribute in honour of the Illustrious Dead.

The Antiquity of the Irish Games.

The earliest authentic records of these great National Games, contained in our ancient manuscripts, are associated with the death and burial of the renowned Queen Tailté, wife of King Eochaidh Mac Erc, the last Firbolg monarch of Erinn.

She was the learned daughter of Mag Mór, a distinguished king of Spain, who reigned in the nineteenth century before the Incarnation; and her husband, Eochaidh (Aughy), was slain in the historic Battle of Moytura, fought between the Firbolgs and the invading colony of Tuatha Dé Danaan, on the plains of Cong, in County Mayo, in 1896 B.C.

This, it may be remarked, is one of the oldest, if not actually the very oldest, events of which authentic records exist in ancient Irish history.

As, however, the mere mention of such bald and otherwise uninteresting dates conveys no adequate idea of their antiquity to the mind of the ordinary reader, it may serve to awaken some additional interest in the subject if we associate them with some of the great outstanding events in the contemporary history of the world.

12

Other Historic Dates compared with Tailteann.

It will, no doubt, surprise some of our readers to learn that the Tailteann Games were instituted and celebrated in ancient Ireland more than a thousand years before the misty, if not mythical, Romulus is supposed to have yoked his oxen and ploughed his legendary furrow around the great circle within which the ancient city of Rome, with its many Cæsars and wonderful history, was subsequently to arise to fame.

Nor was the far-famed city of Troy, of which Homer sings in his *Iliad*, and the story of which has proved an interesting but tearful task to many of us in our schooldays, yet in existence. The Siege of Troy did not occur, as recent research has proved, till more than seven hundred years after Tailté was laid to rest in her mighty *Múr* on the Loch Crew Hills.

The famous Olympian Games, of which we hear so much from time to time, and which, at best, were but a pale reflex of those of Tailteann, were not yet instituted in the sea-girt province of Elis, in ancient Greece, till more than four hundred years after King Lughaidh Lamhfada, or Lewy of the Long Hand, summoned "All the men of Erinn" to celebrate the Tailteann ceremonies on the plains of Royal Meath.

13

Even the Kingdom of Athens itself, subsequently so famed for its learning, its art, and its culture, was not yet founded by Cecrops and his Egyptian colony—although it existed long before the Olympian Games began—till at least more than three hundred years after the woods of Tailteann resounded to the rush and roar of Irish chariots in their thunderous contests for the victor's crown.

Still further away in the dim ages of the past—and perhaps this may illustrate the antiquity of our athletic festival better than all the rest—the games of Tailteann were celebrated in Ireland some three hundred and twenty-five years before Pharaoh's daughter discovered Moses on the banks of the Nile.

Historical Facts.

Unlike the preposterous mythological gods and goddesses, to whom, for want of more inspiring ideals, the Ancient Greeks instituted their games and dedicated their temples, Tailté was a real personage, an ordinary human being, endowed with ordinary human attributes and high accomplishments. She was no impossible myth, such as Minerva, Juno, Jupiter, or imaginary beings of that kind.

14

During her lifetime this distinguished Irish queen had taken the trouble to select a particular spot in which she wished to be buried. It was located on the side of a hill, covered with dense forest; but because of its sunlit and beautiful situation she had chosen it, and her husband, in compliance with her wishes, had it cleared of the timber. It took a host of stalwart men nearly a year to accomplish the task.

In this spot Tailté desired her *Leath*, or tomb, should be made, her *Guba*, or public lamentations, recited, and her *Nosad*, or funeral rites and games, duly celebrated, according to the recognised customs of the country. There was nothing superhuman about such ordinary facts, from which we learn the customs of the people, and how distinguished personages were honoured in Ireland, three thousand years ago.

THE AONACH, A PUBLIC NATIONAL ASSEMBLY.

The institution of an Aonach, or Fair, as it is sometimes misleadingly called, at any particular place, in early pagan times, arose from the burial there of some great or renowned personage, such as a distinguished king or queen, an illustrious warrior chieftain, or a famous man of learning.

On such an occasion a great national assembly was called together, usually by order of the king, to celebrate the funeral rites of the deceased, and at the same time to avail of the gathering to promulgate any improvements or extensions in the established laws of the nation.

When summoned by the *Ard Righ,* or High King, such assemblies were of the greatest national importance, and as such were attended by all the minor kings, chiefs and nobles, as well as by vast multitudes of the people from all parts of the five provinces.

THE THREE FUNCTIONS OF THE AONACH.

As a national institution the Aonach fulfilled three important public functions in the lives of the people. Its first object was, to do honour to the illustrious dead; secondly, to promulgate laws; and, finally, to entertain the people.

The First Function.

The first object was carried out with great solemnity and impressive ceremonies, in which all present played their allotted parts, as strictly prescribed by ancient custom and the law. The *Guba*, or mourning chants, were sung by specially invited guests. The *Cepóg*, which was a strange and beautiful dirge, was sung by the druids and poets attached to the person or court of the deceased. It was initiated by the Chief Druid and taken up and improvised by each singer in turn, and recounted the family history, recited the personal exploits, and lamented the loss of the departed. It was no ordinary expression of regret; and its composition and intonation evinced an art requiring much study, cultivation and practice. Few who have

17

ever heard this weird lament, even as it is sung, or chanted, to-day, can ever forget it.*

Cremation Ceremonies.

After the *Cepóg* was sung by the druids and poets assembled around the bier, some very weird religious ceremonies were gone through. Next morning the body was transferred to an inflammable pile, and at the close of day the torches were lighted at the great fire of the Aonach, and the pyre ignited. Then, as the column of black smoke ascended, the assembled multitude turned their faces to the setting sun, and, raising their right hands aloft, saluted the departing God of Day. These rites occupied from one to three days, according to the rank of the deceased.

* This custom, strange to say, although gradually dying out, still continues in some of the more remote Irish-speaking districts of the south and west, where the true tradition of the ancient *Cepóg* may be heard at the present day. A learned writer describing it says : "I once heard in West Muskerry, in the county of Cork, a dirge of this kind, excellent in point of both music and words, improvised over the body of a man who had been killed by a fall from a horse ; it was chanted by a young man, the brother of the deceased. He first recounted his genealogy; eulogised the spotless honour of his family ; described in the tones of a sweet lullaby his childhood and boyhood; and then, changing the air suddenly, he spoke of his wrestling and hurling; his skill at ploughing ; his horsemanship; his prowess at a fight in a fair ; his wooing and marriage ; and ended by suddenly bursting into a loud, piercing, but exquisitely beautiful wail, which was again and again taken up by the bystanders."

The Second Function.

After the conclusion of the religious ceremonies, on the fourth day the *Ard Righ* took his
place before the royal seat at sun-rise. The minor
kings, princes, nobles, chieftains, and all persons
of title to the twenty-sixth degree, together with
the queens and other noble dames, all took their
prescribed places, to the right and left of the
monarch, whilst the assembled people stood in
silence before him. Then the trumpets blared
forth, the High King turned to the east, saluted
the sun, and the assemblage followed suit.

When the ceremony of saluting the sun was
over, the *Ard Righ,* dressed in his splendid
robes, stood forth and addressed his people.

Having fittingly alluded to " the Illustrious
Dead " whose burial rites they had performed,
he called upon his Arch-Druid, or Chief Ollamh,
to proclaim the Royal Truce for the period of
the Aonach, and promulgate the latest laws
enacted for the realm.

The " Man of Learning " (Ollamh), respond·
ing to the king's command, ascended a mound
and read the laws which he had enshrined in
beautiful poetry. This latter was repeated by the
lesser ollamhs, druids and bards distributed

through the multitude, till all present were familiar with their legal rights and duties, the history of their country, the glories of their king, and the war-like deeds of "the Illustrious Dead." Then another great fire was lighted, and the second function of the Aonach concluded.

The Third Function.

Next came the *Cuiteach Fuait,* or third great function, consisting of the Funeral Games in honour of the dead; and it is curious to note how this ancient custom of rejoicing after a funeral is still practised in many countries. At military funerals in almost all parts of the world, as well as at public funerals generally, after the deceased is laid to rest, the attendant bands cease playing their " Dead Marches," and other lugubrious tunes, and immediately strike up the liveliest airs in their repertoire. Whence this custom came can never be determined, since it existed before history began to be written.

THE GAMES.

The *Cuiteach Fuait*, as these funeral games were called, consisted of athletic, gymnastic and equestrian contests of various kinds, and included running, long-jumping, high-jumping, hurling, quoit-throwing, spear-casting, sword-and-shield contests, wrestling, boxing, swimming, horse-racing, chariot-racing, spear or pole jumping, slinging contests, bow-and-arrow exhibitions, and, in fact, every sort of contest exhibiting physical endurance and skill. In addition, there were literary, musical, oratorical, and story-telling competitions; singing and dancing competitions, and tournaments of all kinds. Also, competitions for goldsmiths, jewellers, and artificers in the precious metals; for spinners, weavers and dyers; and the makers of shields and weapons of war. All were conducted under specially prescribed conditions; and articles of guaranteed home-manufacture were examined and tested with the greatest care.

"The Fair"—Not a Special Function.

Finally, and more as a mere consequence than as a special function, the Aonach partook of the nature of a great market or fair. All kinds of food, merchandise, live-stock, household utensils, cloth, arms, and articles of wearing apparel were on exhibition, as well as for sale. Foreigners were not excluded from the fairs, and it is specially recorded that the Greeks, as distinguished from our less distant foreign neighbours, had special "Great Marts" of their own allotted to them for the sale of precious gems, jewellery, gold ornaments, and many coloured silken cloaks. In fact, merchants and dealers of all kinds availed themselves of these great assemblies, and, exhibiting their wares, appear to have pushed a lively trade.

Such was the character of the ancient Aonaiġ, many of which were held in ancient Ireland long before Rome was founded. The most important, however, were Aonach Tailteann in Meath, Aonach Carman in Wexford, and Aonach Colmain on the Curragh of Kildare.

The Bye-Laws of the Aonach.

All those great gatherings, it should be remembered, were regularly organised assemblies. They were regulated strictly, and in detail, by legally prescribed bye-laws, the transgression of which, in many instances, meant death. A universal truce was proclaimed in the High King's name, and woe betide the man who broke it. No one could be arrested for any previous offence, nor could anyone be distrained, detained, or otherwise vexatiously interfered with, either whilst going to, attending at, or returning from the Aonach. All feuds, fights, quarrels and such-like disturbances were strictly forbidden and severely dealt with; and all known criminals were rigorously excluded from both the games and the assembly. It is interesting to note that almost identical bye-laws were subsequently instituted and enforced at Olympia.

Women Specially Protected.

Under the bye-laws special protection was afforded to women of all classes. They were not, as at Olympia (in this respect only did the latter bye-laws differ from the Irish), excluded from the assembly, but, on the contrary, special features were provided to attract their attendance; and a curious match-making mart and marriage ceremony were established on the grounds. A particular enclosure with stands was provided for their exclusive use, and this was called the *Cot,* or *Cotha,* whence comes the French word *Coterie.*

Elopements Forbidden.

The romance of true love, and the out-manœuvring of unrelenting parents appear to have been rather prevalent in ancient Erinn in those days, since we find elopements, *during the truce,* most rigorously banned, lest the absence of parents or guardians at the Aonach might be availed of by lovers. It was, in fact, deemed " a heinous offence," and the abduction of a lady, *against her will,* brought down the wrath of the monarch himself on the head of the offender. Nevertheless, this offence was not uncommon in Ireland as late as a hundred years ago.

Some Contrasts.

In the foregoing respect, it should be mentioned, the moral obligations in force in

Ireland, at least during these celebrations, were strikingly in contrast with those in ancient Greece, when the Olympian Games were established some hundreds of years later. And as to Ancient Rome, there does not appear to have been any moral obligations imposed on anyone at any time! The *Ludi* of Ancient Rome however, did not come into existence until some eleven hundred years after the institution of Tailteann, and they degenerated rapidly into a carnival of licensed debauchery.

THE ORIGIN OF THE TAILTEANN GAMES.

The story of these ancient Irish games is, shortly, this :—Eochaidh (Aughy) Mac Erc was a famous monarch of Ireland in the very earliest days of her history. He was, in fact, the last King of the Firbolgs, and occupied the throne when the invading colony of Tuatha Dé Danaan landed on our shores more than three thousand eight hundred years ago (1897 B.C.).

Eochaidh advanced from Tara with a host of chiefs and legions of men to expel the invaders who were encamped at Moytura, near Cong, in Co. Mayo, and the king engaged them in battle.

According to St. Colum Cille, this Battle of Moytura (*Magh Tuireadh*) was the most strenuous, if, indeed, not the most amazing, battle recorded in our whole history. It is recorded in mány ancient MSS. and is referred to by O'Curry as one of the first authentic events in our chronological history.   In this battle Eochaidh Mac Erc, the husband of Tailté, was slain.

Irish Intercourse with Spain.

For many years before his death this ancient Firbolg king had been in constant communication, and close business relationship, with Spain, and had married Tailté, the daughter of Magh Mór, a well-known Spanish King.   This royal princess, in whose honour the Tailteann Games were originally instituted, was not only a very beautiful and stately woman, but one of the most learned and accomplished ladies in the whole of Europe.   She is said to have mastered every science, art, and knowledge, not only in Europe, but even in the Eastern World; and to have earned and deserved the reputation of being " the most distinguished druidess in the Western World."

Queen Tailté.

Tailté came to Ireland as the queen of Eochaidh Mac Erc more than nineteen centuries before the Christian era, and took up her abode in the royal palace of Tara. Here she won the universal esteem and admiration of "All the men of Erinn" both for her beauty and wonderful accomplishments. She instructed the *ollamhs* and druids in many arts that redounded to the honour and glory of her adopted country. Under her benign influence peace and harmony reigned throughout the land, until the coming of the Dé Danaan.

Tailté's Tomb.

Some time previous to her husband's death Queen Tailté had personally selected her own burial place. It was a beautifully situated spot on the sun-lit slopes of *Caill Cuain*, in the midst of a great rolling forest. At her request the encircling trees were cut down and removed, and a large area on the green hillside reserved for her *leacht*, or tomb. This spot appeared like a great glistening emerald, reflecting the sunshine from within its sombre setting of surrounding forest. It was truly a beautiful place, and could be seen from the doors of her favourite palace (at Teltown) some twelve miles away. In this spot she had decreed that her *Aonach* should be held, her *Guba* sung, and her *Nosadh* celebrated, when she had passed away.

28

Her Foster-Son—Lugh (Loo).

Fosterage at that time, as in subsequent years, was customary in royal families in Ireland, and Tailté had taken a noble youth of tender years to be fostered at her court. His name was Lugh, or Lugaidh (Louie), Mac Eithleen, and although of the invading race who had slain her husband, she had him brought up most carefully under her own personal instruction. She paid particular care and attention to his education, and taught him every art, science and mystery known to herself; so that when he afterwards ascended the throne, he was one of the most learned men and accomplished warriors in Erinn.

Tailté Laid to Rest.

King Lugh lived at his great palace at Nás (now Naas, in Co. Kildare), and on the death of Tailté at her residence near Teltown, in Co. Meath, he had her interred in her " green circle on the distant hills." She was buried in royal state, with impressive druidical rites, on the side of *Caill Cuain* (now called *Sliabh Caillighe*); her *Guba* was duly sung, and her *Nosadh* celebrated, as she had wished.

29

AN ANCIENT MANUSCRIPT RECORD.

The foregoing facts are recorded in one of our oldest writings, from which the following excerpt is taken as an interesting specimen of ancient Irish composition :—

ON THE ORIGIN OF TAILLTEN.

Taillten, why so called? Answer : Tailtiu, daughter of Madh Mór, the wife of Eochaidh Garbh, son of Duach Temin ; it was by him the 'Mound of the Strangers' at Tara was made ; and she was the foster-mother of Lugaidh, son of Scol Balbh, and it was she that requested her husband to cut down *Caill Cuain*, that there should be an *Aonach* around her *Leacht* (tomb) ; and she died on the Kaland of August after that, and her *Guba* (lamentations) and her *Nosad* (funeral rites and games) were celebrated by Lugadh. *Unde Lug Nosad dicitur.** Five hundred years, moreover, and three thousand before the birth of Christ this occurred , and this assemblage was celebrated by every king who occupied Erinn till Patrick came. And four hundred years it continued to be celebrated in Taillten from Patrick to the Black Fair of Donchad, son of Fland, son of Malachy. Three prohibitions were upon Taillten, namely, to pass through it without alighting ; to see it over the left shoulder ; and to throw a cast (of a spear) in it which does not reach its mark. *Unde* the Fair of Taillten *dicitur*, of which is said the following :—

I.

You nobles of the land of comely Conn,
Listen to us for our blessing ;
Till I relate to you the ancient history
Of the origin of the Aonach Tailtiu.

II.

Tailtiu, daughter of renowned Madh Mór,
Wife of Eochaidh Garbh, son of Duach Dall,
Was thither brought by the Firbolg host
To *Caill Cuain*, after a co-valiant battle.

* Lug Nosad (*i.e.*, Loo Nosa), from which *Lammastide* is derived.

Caill Cuain, tall and stately were its trees
From *Eisgir* to *Ath n-Droman* ;
From *Monad Mor*, of great adventures ;
From *Aill* to *Ard na Suigi*.

From *Suigi* of the *Suighe Sealga*,
Whither went the Companies of *Druim Dearg*.
From the wood eastward the chariot heads did pass
Into *Ath Find* from *Cuil Clochar*.

The confluence of Curach, the head of the river,
The hill of *Banba* where spears are wont to be.
The hounds of Cairpri were triumphant
Over the borders of *Tipra Mungarge*.

Many the heroes of the pagans,
The battles, the battalions, the great fires
That were engaged in felling *Caill Cuainn*,
Delightful was the host of the Firbolgs.

When she had felled the beautiful wood,
And having cleared its roots out of the ground,
Before the end of one year it was *Crieg Muigh*,
It was a flowery plain adorned with shamrocks.

By Order of the King.

On the death of Tailté a great national Aonach
was ordered by King Lugh to solemnise her
funeral rites and institute the commemoration
games already described ; and the *Cuiteach Fuait*,
or funeral games, continued to be celebrated as
an annual celebration on the first of August
(Lammastide) for many centuries.   Occasionally
they were interrupted for one reason or another,
but as time rolled on they were revived again by
succeeding High Kings and on each occasion with

increased splendour, until at length the Aonac Tailteann became one of the greatest and most firmly established institutions in the nation.

A Dress Parade of Kings.

It would be no easy task, indeed, to convey any true or adequate idea, at the present day, of the magnitude and magnificence of this ancient celebration as it continued in its ever-increasing splendour adown the centuries.

Even at that time it had become famous all over Europe. Knowledge of it had extended into ancient Greece, and inspired the institution of the great Olympian Games at Elis, in the year 1222 B.C.

Like to our Irish Horse Show, which has developed from a comparatively small and insignificant gathering into its present dimensions, attended as it is by visitors from all parts of the world, as a parade of fashion, the Tailteann Games ultimately attained gigantic proportions, and became a veritable full-dress parade of kings and queens and royal personages, descending in " grades of honour and nobility to the twenty-sixth degree." It was attended by their long retinues of lords and ladies, chiefs and champions, ollamhs, bards and poets; men of science and of learning, artificers and warriors, each bedizened in his or her particularly distinctive dress of brilliant colours, as prescribed by law.

A Vision of the Past.

It must be remembered that those were the days when personal adornment had reached its climax of superb and royal splendour; when every king and queen and prince and chief, with their attendant lieutenants and personages-in-waiting, presented a veritable pageant of glory in their costumes and apparel. Their head-dresses were either crowns, or crescents, or helmets, of burnished steel, silver, or gold; their adorned hair was interwoven with golden spirals and their plaited locks were pendant with golden balls: their necks were encircled with collars and torques of gold inlaid with sparkling gems and rich enamels. Their beautiful silken cloaks, in rich colours of every shade and hue, hung from their shoulders in flowing folds, and were fastened and held in position with jewelled clasps and great brooches of gold and silver and bronze of exquisite design and workmanship—those beautiful things we now see preserved in the

33

c

Royal Irish Academy or the National Museum. Those were the days when *lenas* or shirts of noble men and women were made of many-coloured Oriental silks, embroidered with threads of silver and of gold, and their sandals and leg-straps were of leather adorned with red enamel and "snow-white bronze": when every king and chief and noble warrior appeared in public bearing a burnished shield, graven with wonderful designs, and embossed with gold, and wearing swords with inlaid and richly jewelled hilts: when their prancing war-steeds were radiantly caparisoned with gold-embroidered draperies, silver collars with tiny golden bells, and jewelled bridles of red enamelled leather.

Conceive, then, the plains of Royal Meath crowded for miles with such a magnificent gathering, and we get some idea of the surpassing splendour of the ancient ᴀonᴀiᵹ. Such were those great National Assemblies in ancient Erinn, long before the dawn of Christianity; and such they continued to be for more than three thousand years, till the days of Roderick O'Connor.

The Last Celebration.

Its last celebration, by the last King of Ireland (A.D. 1169), was, if we are to judge it by the

34

contemporary writers, the greatest and most
impressive of all. We are told :—

"Aonac Taillcen imoppo oo oenain la pig
Epeann ocup la let Chuinn oon cup pin ocup po
letpecc a n- gnaipne ocup mapcpluag o Mullac
Aioi go Mullac Taillcen."

"On this occasion the Aonach Tailteann was
celebrated by the King of Ireland and the people
of Leath-chuinn (the northern half of Ireland);
and their horses and cavalry were spread out on
the space extending from Mullach Aidi to
Mullach Tailteann."

As the distance here given from *Mullach Aidi*
(now Lloyd's Hill), west of Kells, to *Mullach
Tailteann* (now *Sliabh na Cailligh*), at the Royal
Cemetery of Tailteann is a span of more than
seven miles across a beautiful plain in Co. Meath,
and as King Roderick O'Connor was a rigorous
upholder of the formalities and observances of all
Court and State functions, especially as to apparel
and ornamental jewellery, even to the wearing
of silken hose and golden garter-clasps such as
are worn to-day by the Knights of St. Patrick,
we can easily imagine, then, the radiant splendour
and superb magnificence of the last celebration of
Aonach Tailteann.

FINN MacCOOL AT THE AONACH.

The Achilles of Ireland, as we may call the far-famed Irish champion, Finn MacCool, is undoubtedly one of the greatest athletic figures in Irish history. Although tradition and legend have woven around his exploits a fabulous fairy mantle of the wildest impossibilities, he was, nevertheless, a very real and distinguished military commander of unequalled prowess. His real athletic achievements and warlike exploits, as attested by reliable historical records, were not by any means humanly impossible, but some of them, certainly, were such as would put the very best of our modern athletic champions to shame. Nor, indeed, is this to be wondered at when we consider the amazing care and attention paid to physical culture and development in those days, more particularly in the higher grades of society.

36

Even in the lowest grades, amongst the gillie, or servant class, we find men before whose everyday duties the great achievements of our modern " Marathon " champions would pale into insignificance. Those " horse-boys," as they were called, of olden times, could keep up, on foot, with their masters on the swiftest horses, all day long; and repeat the performance each succeeding day till the horses became exhausted.*

Indeed, it was one of the special obligations imposed on the lesser kings, the chiefs and the nobles, by the exacting "Laws of Fosterage," to physically train and intellectually develop every foster-child committed to their care, until the latter could undergo extremely severe tests in every athletic exercise with satisfaction and honour. When compared with these tests our modern athletic contests are mere child's play.

The Fianna Eireann at Tailteann.

In this connection it may be of interest to recall the fact that Aonach Tailteann was an established recruiting centre and testing station, at which Finn MacCool regularly attended with

* See Appendix II., page 69.

his officers, to examine and test all candidates presenting themselves for commissions in his famous legion, the *Fianna Eireann.*

Previous to the establishment of this renowned military legion, under the command of Finn's grandfather, there was no regularly organised army in Ireland to protect and defend the interests and exact the tributes or taxes of the *Ard Righ.* Every chief had his own warriors, and the provincial and local kings were entitled to call upon such chiefs to defend their respective local interests; whilst on great national issues, involving the armed defence of the entire nation, all the lesser kings and chieftains were invited to participate, but there was no regular national army until the time of Finn's grandfather.

When Finn MacCool was appointed to the command of the *Fianna Eireann,* it consisted of several battalions of selected warriors located in the different provinces, under their respective chiefs, who were all tried *Champions* of great war-like prowess. As vacancies occurred in the ranks, they were filled by examinations and tests held at Tailteann, Uisneach, Cruachan and other places, during the games held at those centres, of which Tailteann was the most important.

Here, under the eyes of the assembled multitude the tests were held. The competitors for commissions were summoned by a fanfare of trumpets and were put through their facings under the critical supervision of the *Ard Righ* and their commander, Finn MacCool. To fail was not deemed any disgrace as few, indeed, could reach such a high standard of athletic proficiency.

Previous to Finn's appointment to the command of the legion the only really difficult test was one involving great dexterity with shield and sword in personal defence. The candidate had to defend himself, in real earnest, from the simultaneous attack of no less than nine warriors, the aspirant being armed with spears and sword in addition to his heavy shield. This test, however, seems to have been too easy for the new commander, and he accordingly increased the competitor's task by the addition of ten conditions to the already existing four. Some of these would, we fear, tax the athletic accomplishments of our present day military officers. The fourteen tests were :—

1st. No officer of the Fianna shall accept any fortune with his wife, but shall select her for her moral conduct and accomplishments.

2nd. No member of the legion shall, under any circumstances, insult a woman.

3rd. No member shall refuse any person for trinkets or food.

4th. No member shall turn his back on or fly from nine champions.

These were the original four conditions, which were not sufficiently exacting for Finn, who determined to convert all his soldiers into veritable *Champions*. He accordingly introduced the following ten additional conditions for qualifications into his famous band :—

5th. No man shall be admitted into the Fianna, at the great meetings of Uisneach, nor at the Aonach Tailteann, until his father and his mother, his tribe and his relatives, give security that they shall not avenge his death. So that he shall not expect anyone to avenge him but himself.

6th. No man shall be admitted until he is accomplished and has mastered " The Twelve Books of Poetry."

7th. No man shall be admitted until, standing knee-deep in a wide pit, he has shown that he can protect himself, without receiving a scratch, with his shield and a hazel stake no longer than a man's arm, from the attack of nine warriors, simultaneously hurling their nine spears at him, from a distance of nine ridges.

8th. No man shall be admitted until, his hair being plaited, he has been chased, at a starting distance of one intervening tree, through several forests with a host of Fianna in pursuit and with full intent to wound him, and he has proved himself competent to escape capture or a wound.

9th. No man shall be received in whose hands shall tremble a champion's arms.

10th. No man shall be admitted if a single braid of his hair be loosened out of its plait in his flight through a tangled wood (brushwood, scrub, etc.).

11th. No man shall be admitted whose foot shall break a single withered branch in his flight through a forest.

12th. No man shall be admitted unless he is able to jump over a branch of a tree as high as his forehead, and stoop under one as low as his knee, without delay in his speed, to show his agility.

13th. No man shall be admitted unless he can pluck a protruding thorn from his heel with his hand without hindrance to his speed.

14th. No man shall be admitted until he has first sworn fidelity to the Commander of the Fianna.

THE MARRIAGE MARKET.

An interesting item included in the programme of this ancient assembly was that of
match-making. As an institution, that preroga-
tive of parents has persisted in Ireland even to
the present day. At Tailteann, however,
marriages formed a special feature of the
Aonach, but whether this circumstance was a
particular consequence of the probationary
nature of the " Tailteann Marriage " contract,
or not, it is now impossible to say.

Crowds of youths and maidens from all over
the surrounding districts, " dressed all in their
best," and accompanied by their parents,
attended the Aonach. They were not, however,
permitted, had they not known each other
before, to even make each other's acquaint-
ance; the girls were stowed away in a large
enclosure, and, practically speaking, were com-
pelled to " shut their eyes and open their arms

and take what chance would send them," whilst the young men, probably, strolled about looking at the sports and contests.

The Match-Making.

In the meantime the parents assembled— pretty much as they foregather at the local public-house to-day after a fair—at the sacred mound in the " Marriage Vale," and made suitable, or much more likely unsuitable, matches for their children. The latter, however, were never consulted, and had to take the partners selected for them by their natural guardians. Even some of the delicate duties of the parents on such occasions, such as arranging the marriage portions, or " fortunes " as they are called, were spared them by the laws of the land. The good old laws of those days left nothing of that kind to good nature or chance, or even to the mollifying influence of a " naggin of punch "; they specifically laid down the dowry in proportion to the means and relative ranks or grades of the contracting parties.

The matches having been satisfactorily concluded, the selected couples were led forthwith to the *Tulach-na-Coibche,* or " Mound of the Buying," where the *bride-price* was duly handed over and the ceremony celebrated.

Divorce.

Close to the " Marriage Vale " in which the *Tulach-na-Coibche* stood, there was, curiously enough, a pair of mounds or hillocks, upon which, should any newly-wedded pair regret their lot *within a year and a day*, they could, by going through a curious pagan ceremony, dissolve their unhappy union.

The two mounds, or, at least, all that remains of them, which were known as the " Hills of Separation," are to be seen there to-day. A well-known historian and archæologist who made a very careful and searching examination of the district tells us :—

"About forty perches north-west of the spot pointed out as the ' Vale of Marriage,' two earthen mounds, popularly known as *The Knockans*, but which tradition says constitute the ' Hills of Separation,' still exist. The distance between the bases of the two mounds, which run parallel, is about ten feet, and the gradual slope at each end of both affords an easy means of ascent and descent."

The length of these two mounds is, roughly, about a hundred yards, and their height about thirty feet.

Such were the twin altars of nuptial renunciation upon which the "incompatibilities of
temper" were adjusted by a curious pagan
ceremony, where the united couple "turned
their backs upon one another" for ever.

The husband and wife, having decided
within the allotted time of "a year and a day"
(no longer period was allowed) to dissolve their
union, met at the mounds, on the occasion of
the next annual Aonach; both ascended the
same mound from opposite ends, at the same
time, and, meeting midway on the summit,
questioned each other as to their resolve to part.
Having mutually agreed, they both turned to the
east, facing the rising sun, saluted it, and
the husband, announcing to the assembled
multitude the reasons for their estrangement,
proclaimed his intention to live with his wife
no longer. Then, turning their backs
towards one another, the unhappy couple
walked to opposite ends of the mound
and descended. Next, the second mound
was ascended in like manner from opposite
ends, and the same ceremony gone through;
but on this occasion the wife and husband
turned to the west, saluted the Couch of
the Sun, and the lady made the announcement

renouncing the partner who had been chosen for her and declared she would no longer live with him. Again they turned their backs, descended in opposite directions, and both had achieved their freedom.

This was, apparently, an easy, simple and inexpensive process of divorce, yet, in reality, it was not, by any means, quite so easy as it appears. Circumstances were such, and the moral code so high at that time in pagan Ireland, that a public renunciation of the obligations of one of their most sacred ceremonies required a determination almost heroic, particularly since the probability was that neither party would ever succeed in securing another partner. So that a " Tailteann Marriage " was, in reality, no mere loose and happy-go-lucky union to be indulged in at leisure and broken at will.

OTHER FESTIVE ASSEMBLIES IN ANCIENT IRELAND.

There were several other assemblies, of a somewhat similar nature to Aonach Tailteann, held in Ireland in olden times. They were, however, much more restricted and provincial in their character. They were, indeed, more or less local gatherings of annual occurrence, at which local and general laws were proclaimed, games held, and literary and musical contests adjudicated.

Such, however, was not the case with the assemblies known as *Aonach Cruachan*, celebrated in County Roscommon, and *Aonach Carman*, in Wexford. These partook more or less of the character of National Assemblies, and were generally attended by the Irish kings and nobles of all the provinces. There was also a celebrated gathering known as *Aonach Colmain*, to which we shall have to refer.

AONACH CARMAN.

The site upon which this ancient assembly was held is now occupied by the town of Wexford. Like all the other assemblies of this kind, it originated in the burial there of a famous personage several centuries before the birth of Christ.

The circumstances under which this Aonach was originally established are interesting . in many ways, not the least of which is the fact, recorded in several of our oldest manuscripts, that the Carman in commemoration of whom it was instituted was a Greek lady who came from Athens with her three sons. As recorded in the ancient MS. known as the " Book of Leinster." It runs thus :—

" Carman, why so called? Answer : Three men who came from Athens, and one woman with them, i.e., the three sons of Dibad, son of Dorcha, son of Ainches, i.e., Dian, Dubh, and Dothur were their names, and Carman was the name of their mother."

It was believed by the Tuatha Dé Danaan people who then inhabited Ireland, that this Grecian lady and her three sons exercised some baneful influence in the country which militated against the peace and prosperity of the nation. The people, therefore, determining to put an end to the danger once for all, expelled the sons, but not their mother. As the ancient authority tells us :—

1. "Listen, O Lagenians of the monuments !
   Ye truth-upholding hosts,
   Until you get from me, from every source,
   The pleasant history of the far-famed
   Carman.

2. Carman, the field of a splendid fair,
   With a widespread, unobstructed green
   The hosts who came to celebrate it
   On it they contested their noble races.

3. The renowned field is the cemetery of kings,
   The dearly loved of noble grades;
   There are many meeting mounds,
   For their ever loved ancestral hosts.

4. To mourn for queens and for kings,
   To denounce aggression and tyranny,
   Often were the fair hosts in autumn
   Upon the smooth brow of noble old Carman.

(D480)   D

5. Was it men, or was it a man of great
 valour,
 Or was it a woman of violent jealousy,
 Gave the name, without the merit of noble
  deeds—
 Bestowed the true name of beautiful Carman?

6. It was not men, and it was not a fierce man,
 But a single woman, fierce, rapacious,
 Great her rustling and her tramp,
 From whom Carman received its first name.

7. Carman, the wife of the fierce Mac Dibad,
 Son of Dorcha, of legions and choice hospi-
 tality,
 The son of Ancges, of rich rewards,
 The renowned hero of many battles.

8. They sought not the profits of industry,
 Through ardent love of noble Banba,
 For they were at all times toilers in the
 East—
 The sons of Mac Dibad and their mother.

9. At length they westward came,
 Dian and Dubh and Dothur,

From delightful Athens westward,
'And' Carman their mother.

10. They used to destroy upon the Tuatha Dé—
The wicked malignant race—
The produce of every land unto the shore;
It was a great, an oppressive evil.

11. Carman by all-powerful spells
Destroyed every growing productive fruit,
After each unlawful art being tried
By the sons, with violence, with injustice.

12. Soon as the Tuatha Dé perceived
What deprived them of their summer bloom,
For every evil deed which they wrought,
They hurled an equal deed upon them.

13. Critenbel, he was a Sab,
And Lug Laibech, son of Cachir;
Becuille in every field entangled them
And Ai, the son of Ollam.

14. They said to them when they arrived—
The four warriors of equal valour—
Here is a woman instead of your mother,
Three men for your three brothers.

15. Death to ye we choose not, nor desire,
    It is neither our pleasure nor free choice;
    Assign with openness a proper pledge,
    And depart out of Eriu each of you three.

16. Those men then from us departed—
    They were expelled with great difficulty;
    Though a woman of theirs they left there
    Carman, alive in her narrow cell.

17. Every oath from which there is no release—
    Sea, fire, heaven, and the fair-faced earth—
    That in power or weakness they never would
        return,
    As long as the sea encircled Eriu.

18. Carman, who gave death and battles,
    Once so destructive with her spells,
    Received her fate, as she so well deserved,
    Among the oaks of these firm mounds.

19. Hither came to celebrate her funeral rites,
    To lament her, to inaugurate her Guba,
    The Tuatha Dé, upon the noble, beautiful
        plain;
    This was the first regular Aonach Carman.

20. The grave of Carman, by whom was it dug?
    Will you learn, or do you know?
    According to all our beloved forefathers
    It was Bre, son of Eladan.   Listen!"

The ancient historical poem from which the foregoing stanzas are taken, contains seventy-nine such verses, giving full and accurate details over every circumstance associated with Aonach Carman.   It enumerates the royal personages, and their retinues, etc., who attended this great Fair every third year, together with an account of all the various contests, literary, musical, athletic, horse-racing, etc., as well as the vast numbers of people, steeds, chariots, chieftains, champions and athletes in attendance. Unfortunately, it is much too long to quote in full. As a further example of the detailed historic account, however, we include the following verses giving a list of some of those who attended the celebration :—

37." Sixteen kings to me have been recorded,
    By every Sai, and profound historian,
    From Carman of the branchy harbours,
    Who brought hosts into the noble Aonach.

38. Eight from the populous Dodder—
    Renowned hosts ever to be boasted of—
    They celebrated the regular fair of Carman
    With pomp, and with bright arms.

39. Twelve, without an error in the counting,
    . Of festive fairs I acknowledge
    To the fierce champion of valour ··
    · Of the regal race of the noble Maistiu."

: Any person breaking the Bye-Laws during
the Aonach was severely dealt with, as we are
told :—

56." Whoever transgresses the law of the
        assembly—
    Which Benen with accuracy indelibly
        wrote—
    Cannot be spared on family composition,
    But he must die for his transgression."

And again, the nature of the competitions :—

57." These are the many great privileges—
    Trumpets, harps, wide-mouthed horns,
    Cuisig, timpanists without weariness,
    Poets and petty rhymesters.

58. Fenian tales of Find—an untiring entertain-
        ment—
    Destructions, cattle-preys, courtships,
    Inscribed tablets, and books of trees,
    Satires and sharp-edged runes;

59. Proverbs, maxims, royal precepts
    And the truthful instruction of Fithal,
    Occult poetry, topographical etymologies,
    The precepts of Cairpri, and of Cormac;

60. The Fessa, with the great Feis of Tara
    Fairs, with the Aonach of Emania,
    Annals there are verified,
    Every division into which Eriu was divided.

61. The history of the household of Tara—not
        insignificant,
    The knowledge of every territory in Eriu,
    The history of the women of illustrious
        families,
    Of Courts, Prohibitions, Conquests.

62. The noble testament of Cathair the Great
    To his descendants, to direct the steps of
        rule.
    Each one sits in his lawful place
    So that all attend to them and listen. Listen!

63. Pipes, fiddles, chainmen,
    Castanette-players and tube players,
    A crowd of babbling painted masks,
    Roarers and loud bellowers.

64. They all exert their utmost powers
    For the magnanimous monarch of the
        Barrow,
    Until the noble king, in proper measure,
        bestows
    Upon each art its rightful meed."

Like that of Tailteann this Aonach became
an institution of wide repute throughout the
Europe of those days. It was attended by kings
and nobles and all classes, from all parts of
Ireland, and had a market for the rare and costly
products of the East.

The records dealing with this Aonach all
refer to its origin as having been instituted to
perpetuate the memory of Carman, the Greek
lady from Athens, and state that many Greek
merchants attended the assembly, centuries
before the beginning of the Christian era.

AONACH COLMAIN.

THE CURRAGH RACES.

In olden times—in fact, long before the period of which we have any historical knowledge—it would seem that horse-racing must have been a popular pastime in Ireland.

Standing on the very edge of nebulous historic time, and listening to the voice of Tradition as it floats in to us from the uncharted ocean of the past, its sweetest songs are full of racing steeds and marvellous riders, contesting for wonderful trophies of unheard of beauty. Even our very oldest reliable records are full of glowing accounts of this glorious " pastime of kings," all of which testimony goes to prove that racing in Ireland is " as old as the hills."

In pagan times it became part of the highest conception of the pleasures of *Tir-na-n-Oge*, or the Land of Eternal Youth. Some of our oldest traditional tales, in recounting the joys of that " Land beyond the Grave," tell us that the spirits dwelling there race their wonderful steeds along the shore on the Plain of Sports, in contests with golden currachs on the silver sea.

The traditional love for horse-racing may account for this popular sport continuing its unbroken record at the Curragh since its original institution there at the Aonach Colmain, long before the birth of Christ. At what date this Aonach was originally established is not quite clear, but our ancient records (*Bruden Da Derga*) tell us that Conari, King of Ireland in the first century before Christ, once went with four chariots to the *Cluichi*, or Games, at the Cuirrech Lifé (the Curragh of the Liffey or Kildare).

In olden times this famous race-course was known as the "Curragh of the Liffey," and it was then, as it is to-day, the most celebrated race meeting in Ireland. The very word *Cuirreach* itself, according to the ancient *Glossary of Cormac of Cashel*, signifies *race-course*.

Aonach Colmain was held as an annual assembly on the Curragh, and it was attended then, as it is now, by people from all parts of Ireland. The races were always formally opened by the king, or one of the princes of Leinster acting on behalf of the monarch, and they usually lasted for several days. The king's palace was built at Knockaulin on the edge of the race-course, and the Ard Righ himself distributed the prizes to the winners.

Chariot Races at the Curragh.

Some of the most picturesque and exciting events in the programme of sports at these great gatherings was the Chariot Races. These contests, which were the oldest of their kind in Europe, were conducted under strict rules, sometimes with two horses, sometimes with four, and the owners sat in their chariots beside their standing charioteers, who were the most daring and reckless drivers, but capable of accomplishing wonderful achievements with their splendid horses.

The charioteers, dressed in their gaudy costumes with short cloaks, or capes, of different colours, resembling modern Spanish toreadors, stood erect behind their foaming steeds, and held them in with elaborately decorated reins, studded with red enamel, silver, and gold discs. The pace was furious, and, as they dashed along the course, wheel to wheel, and neck-and-neck with their competitors, clouds of foam and dust rose into the air and almost hid them from view. It must have been a glorious sight to see a Colmain Chariot Race !

But all other tastes were equally well catered for. The horse-racing was pretty much as it is to-day, but no saddles were used, and a single rein passing back between the horse's ears sufficed, with a guiding whip, to pilot them on the course.

There were, also, intellectual competitions which, though less exciting, were none the less keenly contested. The poets and musicians and story-tellers had their programme here as at Tailteann and Carmañ, and recited or played their compositions in public. The outstanding features of these competitions were the odes, epics, and exciting rhapsodies of the poets; the story-tellers' tales of war-like deeds, adventures and courtships; and the marvellous, if, indeed, not magical, compositions of the bards, whose musical strains produced laughter or tears or slumber, as the performer wished.

> " They all exerted their utmost powers
> For the magnanimous *Righ Berba*
> Until the noble king, in proper measure,
>   bestows
> Upon each art its rightful meed."

Such were the famous assemblies of ancient Eire. May we live to see them renewed once more in modern Ireland !

APPENDIX I.

THE IRISH ORIGIN OF THE OLYMPIC GAMES.

It is not generally known, and will, no doubt, surprise many of our otherwise enlightened readers to learn that the far-famed Olympic Games of Ancient Greece drew the inspiration from the still much more ancient games in Ireland. The Hellenic games may, indeed, be traced almost directly to the great national celebrations of Tailteann, Carman and Colmain, not only as their source of origin, but as their models for development. So much so, in fact, that not merely the idea of the games, but the actual games themselves, their sequence at the festivities, the rules under which the various contests were held, and even the very bye-laws, regulating the conduct of the people before, during, and immediately after the celebrations, were all borrowed *en masse* from those already in operation in this country. As Mommsen tells us, it falls to the lot of most nations, in the early stages of their development to be taught and trained by some rival sister nation; so it fell to the lot of Greece to acquire a knowledge of the manners, customs, and social life generally of Ancient Ireland.

In the pre-heroic period of Greece her people were practically composed of two classes: the pastoral inhabitants occupying the interior, mountainous portion of the country, and the commercial or seafaring community, who inhabited the towns and cities on the low-lying sea-board. The latter were the greatest navigators, and most adventurous people in Europe in those days, and their trading vessels left no part of the Western World unvisited in search of commerce. Hence it is we find frequent historical references to Greek traders as having visited Ireland, and established special marts at the various Aonaigh in this country, where, we are told, they disposed of their golden ornaments, jewels, and many-coloured silken cloaks.

That there was a close and even intimate intercourse between the two countries even before the great Olympic Games were established there can be no doubt. In several of our ancient

historical MSS.—documents of great antiquity
still preserved in the libraries of Trinity College
and the Royal Irish Academy, in Dublin, as well
as in various libraries on the Continent—there
are numerous references to the Greeks and their
trading in Ireland.   For example :—

> "Τρι μαρξαιο ριn τιρ τρεoραιξ :—
> Μαρξαο bιo, μαρξαο beo cραι,
> Μαρξαιo μoρ nα n-ξαll n-ξρεξαċ
> 1 m-bιo oρ ιρ αρo έċαċ."

" Three markets in that auspicious country :
A market of food, a market of live stock,
And a great market of the foreign Greeks
Where gold and noble clothes were wont to
be."

The ancient poem from which the foregoing
is taken was written in explanation of the
origin of Aonach Carman (now Wexford). It
tells us how that celebrated assembly, with all its
ceremonies and games, was instituted in commemoration of a distinguished Greek lady who,
with her three sons, "From delightful Athens
westward came," at a period anterior to the date
given by Strabo as that of the institution of the
Olympic Games. So we have it very clearly

established that not only did distinguished personages come to Ireland from Greece, at that very remote period in our history, but that enterprising merchants and traders from that distant land were sufficiently familiar with our country to visit it regularly for the express purpose of disposing of their precious wares at our great national assemblies.

It is through the medium of such travellers and seafaring communities that widely separated nations have, at all times, acquired a knowledge of the culture and borrowed the customs of one another; and it was thus, undoubtedly, that the Greeks became acquainted with the games associated with the burial of the " Illustrious Dead " in Ancient Ireland.

If further proof were needed, we have it in the games themselves. We find all the Irish games, even to hurling, copied and reproduced under similar conditions at the Hellenic celebrations; at least, all with the remarkable exception of the equestrian games, which were not only not popular in Greece, but were actually disliked by the people. In fact, anything with a horse in it was, at that early period, practically *taboo* to them; and from the very earliest times the horse was the bogey or hobgoblin of the Greeks. Even in Homer's famous description of the chariot race at the funeral games of Patroclus, a certain dread of the beautiful steeds may be detected.

Hence it was from this dread of horses, no doubt, that the chariot-racing, which played so prominent a part in the Irish games, were entirely omitted from the early Olympic Games; and, indeed, were not introduced for some centuries. So, also, with the horse-racing, which was not included in the Olympic programme until much later still and never became popular.

So that with the exception of the equestrian items, the games and other ceremonies included in the celebrations were, during the earliest period, practically identical at both the Tailteann and the Olympic festivities, which conclusively shows that the latter were clearly borrowed from their Irish prototypes.

K

APPENDIX II.

THE MARATHON RACE.

One of the most interesting events in modern athletics is the *Marathon Race*. It is a test of three of the highest athletic attributes, *viz.*, Speed, Endurance, and Judgment, any two of which, without the third, will not enable a competitor to achieve success.

This event is of comparatively recent introduction in the athletic world, having originated in Athens at the first of the modern Olympic Games in 1896; and since those International Games only occur every four years, there have been but six Marathon Races held up to the present, *viz.* :

1896, at Athens; 1900, at Paris; 1904, at St. Louis; 1908, at London; 1912, at Stockholm; 1916, (none); 1920, at Antwerp.

There was no *Olympiad* held in 1916 in consequence of the war.

Its Name.

The *Marathon Race* derives its classic name, as most people are no doubt aware, from a remarkable incident associated with the historic battle of Marathon. This famous battle was fought in Greece, on the plain from which it takes its name, between the Greeks and Persians, some 490 years before the birth of Christ.

The Persians, encouraged by numerous previous successes, had contemplated, and had actually undertaken, the wholesale invasion of Europe, and had reached Greece in their onward march. The Greeks realised the danger, and, although outnumbered by ten to one, they assembled their united forces under Miltiades, and engaged the Persians in what was, perhaps, one of the most momentous battles in Europe.

They not only gained the victory, but inflicted such a crushing defeat on the invading Oriental hordes that their power was completely broken, and their designs effectually frustrated for ever.

At that time mounted couriers were not used to carry despatches as they are to-day; and military leaders were always accompanied by a corps of well-trained runners to carry their messages. Hence, according to custom, a runner was immediately despatched from Marathon to Athens with news of the great victory.

The courier, aroused to enthusiasm by the wonderful, and anxiously waited for tidings he bore, ran all the way at top speed, and dropped dead on its delivery. It is in commemoration of this historic run that the *Marathon Race* derives its name.

Long-Distance Couriers.

The distance of the Marathon Race is 42 kilometres, or about 26 statute miles, but it was not the distance that proved too much for the ill-fated courier, it was his excessive speed.

In fact, fifty, or a hundred, or even two hundred miles, was not anything unusual for an army courier in those days. The *Peichs*, or Persian couriers of the Turkish sultans, often ran from Constantinople to Adrianople and back, a distance of some 220 miles, in two days and nights, without any untoward effects, and it is interesting to note that they carried silver beads in their mouths to allay their thirst during their runs.

As stated above, the Marathon Race was instituted by the Greeks when the first modern Olympic Games were held at Athens. It was a most appropriate tribute in commemoration of a distinguished fellow-countryman, and it is no less worthy of note that on this occasion also the victorious competitor was a Greek peasant.

Dorando Pietri's Failure.

As an interesting instance of how speed and endurance, uncontrolled by good judgment, failed to win the coveted trophy, the Marathon contest held in connection with the Olympic Games in London in 1908 may be mentioned. It created an immense sensation at the time, and excited the admiration and sympathy of the world.

The race was from Windsor to the Stadium grounds in the Franco-British Exhibition in London, and the first competitor to arrive was an Italian named Dorando Pietri. His condition of physical collapse, however, was such that, appearing to be on the point of death, he had to be assisted over the last few yards of the course. It was hard luck, but according to the conditions he was disqualified, and J. Hayes, an American, was adjudged the winner. A special prize was, however, presented to Dorando Pietri by Queen Alexandra, with universal approval.

APPENDIX III.

THE SPORT RECORDS OF THE WORLD.

Archery.—

Distance, 310 yards. Major Straker (England), 1897.

Billiards (B.C.C. Rules).—

2,196 (unfinished). G. Gray (London), March 17th, 1911.

Billiards (B.A.). —

Cradle Cannon, 499,135. T. Reece, 3rd June to 6th July, 1907.

Cricket.—

Highest Innings: 918: N.S.W. *v.* Australia (Sydney), June 5th—9th, 1901.

Individual Scores (First Class): 424. A. C. MacLaren (Taunton), July 16th, 1895.

Ball Throw: 140 yards. R. Percival (Durham, Sands Australia), Easter Monday, 1884.

Cycling.—

One Hour: Push-bike motor (paced), 63 miles 256 yards.   P. Guignard (Munich), July 1909.

One Mile : Standing start (unpaced).   2 minutes 3 seconds.   Vic. Johnson (Crystal Palace), 1907.

Discus Throw.—

156 feet $11\frac{1}{3}$ inches. A. Taipale (Finland). Madgeburg July 20th, 1913.

Hammer Throw.—

189 feet $6\frac{1}{7}$ inches. P. Ryan (U.S.A.). August 17th, 1913.

Horse Racing.—

One Mile : 1 minute 33 seconds. "Caiman" (Lingfield), July 13th, 1900.

Horse Trotting.—

One Mile : 1 minute 58 seconds.   " Uhlan Lexington " (U.S.A.), October 9th, 1912.

Hurdle Racing.—

120 Yards : $14\frac{3}{5}$ seconds. E. J. Thomson (Philadelphia, U.S.A.), May 29th, 1920.

Javelin Throw.—

216 feet 3 inches. J. Myrra (Finland).

Jumping.—

High Jump : 6 feet 7⅝ inches. E. Beeson (California), May 2nd, 1914.

Long Jump : 25 feet 3 inches. E. Gourdin (Harvard, U.S.A.), July, 1921.

Pole Jump : 13 feet 5 inches. F. K. Foss (Antwerp), August 20th, 1920.

Motor Cycling.—

One Mile : 35⅗ seconds. J. A. MacNeal (Omaha, U.S.A.), October 4th, 1914.

One Hour : 88 miles 350 yards. L. Humiston (Los Angelos, U.S.A.), January 7th, 1912.

Motor Racing.—

One Mile : 29.01 seconds. Beuz (Brooklands), January 22nd, 1914.

Fifty Miles : 27 minutes 2.33 seconds. Talbot, October 27th, 1913.

One Hour : 112 miles 1,689 yards. De Palma (Sheepshead Bay, U.S.A.), November 16th, 1917.

Running.—

100 Yards : 9⅜ seconds. J. Donaldson (Johannesburg), February 12th, 1910.

Running—(continued):

220 Yards: $21\frac{1}{5}$ seconds. W. R. Applegate (England), B. J. Wefers, R. C. Craig, D. F. Lippincott, H. P. Drew and G. Parker (all U.S.A.).

440 Yards: 47 seconds. M. W. Long (Guttenberg, New Jersey), October 4th, 1900.

880 Yards: 1 minute $52\frac{1}{5}$ seconds. J. E. Meredith (Philadelphia), May 13th, 1916.

One Mile: 4 minutes $12\frac{3}{5}$ seconds. N. S. Tober (Cambridge), July 16th, 1916.

Four Miles: 19 minutes $23\frac{2}{5}$ seconds. A. Shrubb (Glasgow), June 13th, 1904.

Ten Miles: 50 minutes $40\frac{3}{5}$ seconds. A. Shrubb (Glasgow), November 5th, 1904.

One Hour: 11 miles 1.442 yards. J. Bouin (France), Stockholm, July 6th, 1913, Marathon.

Skating.

500 Metres: $43\frac{2}{5}$ seconds. O. Mathieson (Davos), January 17th, 1914.

1,000 Metres: 1 minute $34\frac{4}{5}$ seconds. O. Mathieson (Davos), January 31st, 1909.

One Mile: 2 minutes $27\frac{1}{5}$ seconds. F. W. Dix (Cowbit), February 6th, 1912.

Swimming (Bath).—

50 Yards: $23\frac{2}{5}$ seconds. D. Kahanamoku (San Francisco), 1916.

Swimming—(continued) :

100 Yards: 53 seconds. D. Kahanamoku (Honolulu), September 5th, 1917.

220 Yards: 2 minutes $21\frac{3}{5}$ seconds. N. Ross (San Francisco), November 26th, 1916.

440 Yards: 5 minutes $14\frac{3}{5}$ seconds. N. Ross (Los Angelos), October 9th, 1919.

One Mile: 23 minutes $16\frac{4}{5}$ seconds. B. B. Kiernan (Sydney, N.S.W.).

Walking.—

One Mile: 6 minutes 22 seconds. G. Cummings (Manchester), August 4th, 1913.

Seven Miles: 50 minutes $44\frac{4}{5}$ seconds. G. Goulding (N. Brunswick, U.S.A.), October 23rd, 1915.

One Hour: 8 miles 438 yards. G. E. Larner, September 30th, 1905.

Twelve Hours: 73 miles 145 yards. E. C. Horton, May 2nd, 1914.

Weight Putting.—

16 lbs.: 51 feet. R. W. Rose (U.S.A.), San Francisco, August 21st, 1909.

CHAMPIONS, 1921.

At *Billiards.*—T. Newman.

At *Boxing.*—Jack Dempsey (U.S.A.).

At *Chess.*—Senor Capablanca (World).

At *Cricket (Batting).*—P. Mead.

At *Cricket (Bowling).*—E. R. Wilson.

At *Cycling.*—Moeskops (Holland).

At *Golf.*—Jock Hutchison (U.S.A.).

At *Hammer Throwing.*—P. Ryan (U.S.A.).

At *Hurdle Racing.*—E. J. Thompson (Canada).

At *Jumping (High).*—R. W. Landon (U.S.A.).

At *Lawn Tennis.*—W. T. Tilden (U.S.A.).

At *Rifle Shooting.*—Sergeant Cunningham, R.A.O.C.

At *Running (100 Yards).*—R. W. Applegate (England).

At *Running (1 Mile).*—A. G. Hill (England)

At *Sculling.*—E. Barry (England).

At *Skating.*—O. Mathieson (Norway).

At *Swimming.*—N. Ross (U.S.A.).

At *Walking.*—Frigerio (Italy).

Lightning Source UK Ltd.
Milton Keynes UK
UKHW021834160123
415467UK00005B/149